D0460721

115509416

STANLEY AND LIVINGSTONE
Expeditions through Africa

BEYOND THE HORIZONS

STANLEY AND LIVINGSTONE
Expeditions through Africa

Clint Twist

RSVP

RAINTREE
STECK-VAUGHN
PUBLISHERS

The Steck-Vaughn Company

Austin, Texas

Series editor: Su Swallow
Editor: Nicola Barber, Shirley Shalit
Designer: Neil Sayer
Production: Jenny Mulvanny
Consultant: Gary Moulton, University of Nebraska, Professor Andrew Roberts and Dr. Kevin Shillington

Maps and Illustrations: Brian Watson, Linden Artists

Library of Congress Cataloging-in-Publication Data

Twist, Clint.
  Stanley and Livingstone: expeditions through Africa / Clint Twist.
     p.   cm. — (Beyond the horizons)
  Includes bibliographical references and index.
  ISBN 0-8114-3976-3
  1. Stanley, Henry M. (Henry Morton), 1841-1904.
2. Livingstone, David, 1813-1873.   3. Explorers — Africa, Sub-Saharan — Biography — Juvenile literature.   4. Explorers — Great Britain — Biography — Juvenile literature.   5. Africa, Sub-Saharan — Discovery and exploration — Juvenile literature.   I. Title.   II. Series: Beyond the horizons.
  DT351.S9T85   1995
  916.704'23'0922—dc20   94-21642
                                                    CIP AC

Printed in Hong Kong
Bound in the United States

1 2 3 4 5 6 7 8 9 0 LB 99 98 97 96 95 94

Acknowledgments

For permission to reproduce copyright material the author and publishers gratefully acknowledge the following:

Cover (top left) Yoruba beaded artifact: University of California Museum of Cultural History/The Bridgeman Art Library, (top middle) Kota figure: Bonhams, London/The Bridgeman Art Library, (top right) sketch map of the Victoria Falls: Royal Geographical Society, London, (bottom left) lion: Lanting/ZEFA, (bottom right) Stanley's pith helmet: Royal Geographical Society, London.
Title page Hulton Deutsch Collection Limited
page 4 (left) Royal Geographical Society, London/The Bridgeman Art Library, (right) Hulton Deutsch Collection Limited, (bottom) Gerald Cubitt/Bruce Coleman Limited **page 5** (top) Rob Cousins/Robert Harding Picture Library **page 6** (top) Hulton Deutsch Collection Limited, (bottom) e.t. archive **page 7** e.t. archive **page 8** Science Museum, London/The Bridgeman Art Library **page 9** (left) e.t. archive, (right) C. Bradley/Royal Geographical Society, London **page 10** Royal Geographical Society, London **page 11** (left) Hulton Deutsch Collection Limited, (right) Royal Geographical Society **page 13** Hutchison Library **page 14** (top) Stefano Amantini/Bruce Coleman Limited, (bottom) Royal Geographical Society, London **page 15** (top) Peter Newark's Historical Pictures, (bottom) Dorothy Middleton Collection/Royal Geographical Society, London **page 16** Royal Geographical Society **page 17** Kim Taylor/Bruce Coleman Limited **page 19** W.T. Miller/Frank Lane Picture Agency **page 20** Mary Evans Picture Library **page 21** (left) Marcel Isy-Schmwar/The Image Bank, (right) Guido Alberto Rossi/The Image Bank **page 22** (top) Mark van Aardt/Spectrum Colour Library, (bottom) Royal Geographical Society, London **page 23** Royal Geographical Society, London/The Bridgeman Art Library **page 24** (top) Helene Rogers/Trip (bottom) Royal Geographical Society, London **page 25** Hulton Deutsch Collection Limited **page 27** Hulton Deutsch Collection Limited **page 28** (top) Gerald Cubitt/Bruce Coleman Limited, (bottom) Ann Ronan Picture Library **page 29** (top) Royal Geographical Society, London, (bottom) Hulton Deutsch Picture Library **page 30** e.t. archive **page 31** (top) Robert Harding Picture Library, (bottom) Royal Geographical Society, London/The Bridgeman Art Library **page 32** Adrian Arbib/Royal Geographical Society, London **page 33** (top) Alaistair Laidlaw/Royal Geographical Society, London (bottom) Christer Fredriksson **page 34** Image Select, **page 35** (top) R.W.G. Grenfell/Royal Geographical Society, London, (bottom) The Mansell Collection **page 36** (top) Gerald Cubitt/Bruce Coleman Limited, (bottom) Museum of Mankind, London/The Bridgeman Art Library **page 37** Sarah Errington/Hutchison Library **page 38** (top) Guido Alberto Rossi/The Image Bank, (bottom) The Bridgeman Art Library **page 39** Gerald Cubitt/Bruce Coleman Limited **page 41** Hulton Deutsch Collection Limited **page 42** Hulton Deutsch Collection Limited **page 43** (left) Richard Haynes Trip, (right) Trip.

Contents

Introduction

A famous partnership

David Livingstone and Henry Stanley have become one of the most famous partnerships in the history of exploration. But, in fact, the two men met only once and spent just a few months together. What made their meeting famous was that it took place in the middle of Africa.

Both Livingstone and Stanley were great explorers, leading expeditions right across Africa, along mighty rivers, through dense forests, swamps, and woodland. Of course, their explorations took them through lands that were already well-known to the local African inhabitants. But, through their travels, they revealed Africa to the rest of the world.

David Livingstone (above). This portrait was painted during Livingstone's last visit to Britain, about ten years before he died. Henry Stanley (above right) during the period when he became known as the "smasher of rocks."

Before the expeditions of Livingstone and Stanley, most of Africa south of the Sahara Desert was unknown to Europeans. Beginning in 1841, Livingstone started to fill out the details of the geography of African lakes, rivers, and mountains. He was the first European to set eyes on the magnificent waterfall he named Victoria Falls. Later, Stanley completed the task of exploring and mapping the river systems of Africa.

Although the names Livingstone and Stanley are closely linked, the two men were very different. David Livingstone was inspired by a strong religious faith. He believed that the purpose of his life was to travel and make possible the spread of Christianity. Apart from a few brief visits to Britain, he spent all his adult life in Africa. His experiences in Africa made him an enemy of the slave trade, and he was outspoken in the fight against slavery right up until his death in Africa in 1873. Within a year of Livingstone's death, the main slave market in Zanzibar was closed.

In contrast to Livingstone, Henry Stanley traveled in search of fame and fortune. He first went to Africa as a newspaper reporter. When he "found" Livingstone, the story made headlines around the world, and Stanley became famous. He returned to Africa as a professional explorer, and became the first white person to follow the River Congo (now also known as the Zaïre River) to the Atlantic Ocean. Later, Stanley was employed by the Belgian king, who wanted to create an empire in Africa.

Both explorers had to cross natural barriers such as mountains and swamps during their travels in Africa.

Horizons

After reading this book, you may want to find out more about Livingstone and Stanley, and their world. At the end of some of the chapters you will find **Horizons** boxes. These boxes contain the names of people, places, and things that do not appear elsewhere in the book, but which are connected with the story of Livingstone and Stanley. By looking up these names in the indexes of other reference books, you will discover more about Livingstone and Stanley and their world.

Invasion of Africa

As well as having their place in the history of exploration, the expeditions led by Livingstone and Stanley also mark a turning-point in the history of Africa. Before Livingstone made his first African journey, only small parts of the continent had been claimed by foreign nations. Arab and European merchants traded for gold, slaves, and ivory through a few small territories around the coast. However, by the time Stanley made his last expedition, the so-called "Scramble for Africa" was well under way. Within 60 years of Livingstone's first setting foot in Africa, European nations had laid claim to virtually the whole of the continent.

The Historical Background

Child worker

The house in which David Livingstone was born in 1813. This photo was taken about 60 years after he left home.

David Livingstone was born on March 19, 1813, at Blantyre, on the outskirts of Glasgow, Scotland. His father was a wandering tea peddler, who earned a poor living by selling packets of tea to farms and cottages. The family lived in a small apartment building next to a cotton mill (cotton cloth factory). All of the Livingstone family, David, his two brothers, two sisters and his parents, lived in a single room that measured just 16.5 feet by 10 feet. Although such conditions seem harsh today, at the time this type of housing was considered to be reasonably comfortable for working people. The owner of the cotton mill, who built the apartments, had a reputation for caring for his workers.

David went to work in the mill when he was ten years old. He worked from six o'clock in the morning to eight o'clock at night. His job was to walk around the looms (weaving machines), tying up loose threads. During a day's work, David walked about 18 miles. After work, he either went to evening classes or read books at home. Although David's father was poor he was well-educated, and he encouraged David to study. David's father was also very religious. The family belonged to an independent Protestant sect, and from an early age David and the other Livingstone children were taken regularly to church meetings.

David realized that his future depended on getting a good education, and he worked hard at passing examinations. In 1836, he applied to medical school in Glasgow and was accepted. While he was a medical student, he became interested in the London Missionary Society, which sent missionaries (Christian teachers) overseas to convert people to Christianity. Livingstone became convinced that he was meant to be a medical missionary, and he set his heart on going to China. After passing his medical exams, he applied to the missionary society.

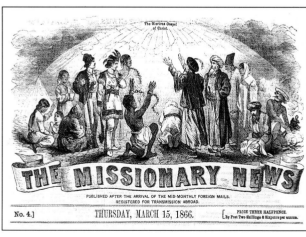

The front of a missionary newspaper, illustrating how Christianity was being spread to all the peoples of the world.

The society accepted David, and he underwent religious training and was ordained as a minister. However, the society decided not to send him to China, but to southern Africa instead.

An abandoned child

The boy who was to become Henry Stanley was born in a small town in North Wales in Great Britain, on January 28, 1841. His name was registered as John Rowlands. His mother was an unmarried teenager and did not want to look after a baby, so she left him with her father. He died when John was five years old, and the boy's other relatives soon abandoned him to the "workhouse."

In 19th-century Britain the homeless, the unemployed, the elderly, and the needy could all get food and shelter at the workhouse — provided they worked for it. Conditions were very harsh: the work was hard, the food bad, and everybody slept in overcrowded dormitories. However, children did receive a little basic education.

John Rowlands did not like the workhouse, and when he was 15, he left. He went to the port of Liverpool where he managed to get a job as a cabin boy on a ship sailing to America. The ship sailed to New Orleans, at the mouth of the Mississippi River, and young John went ashore. He was given a job as a shop assistant by a local businessman, named Henry Stanley. Later he would claim that the businessman adopted him, but this never happened. In 1862, John Rowlands joined the army and fought on the Confederate side in the American Civil War.

In his first battle, John was wounded and taken prisoner. In return for his freedom he agreed to join the opposing Union side, but became ill before he could fight again. After he recovered, he worked as a seaman and then decided to become a journalist. Now calling himself Henry Stanley, he traveled to the frontier of the American West in search of adventure.

Although he sometimes invented parts of his news stories, Henry Stanley soon acquired a reputation as a good journalist. In 1867, he was hired by one of the largest American newspapers, the *New York Herald*, and was sent to Ethiopia (then called Abyssinia) in Africa as a war reporter. Stanley was soon promoted to full-time foreign correspondent based in Europe. In 1871, the *Herald*'s editor decided to send Stanley to look for Livingstone.

A modern world

By 1841, the year that Stanley was born and Livingstone first set foot in Africa, the "modern age" had arrived. In Britain and parts of Europe and North America, the Industrial Revolution was well under way. Nations were now building their wealth on industry and manufactured goods, rather than on agricultural produce.

A cartoonist's view of life in an American frontier town – conditions were often quite primitive.

During the Industrial Revolution, towns and cities grew rapidly in size as more and more factories were built. Hundreds of thousands of people left their traditional jobs in the countryside and moved to the towns where they could get better-paid work in the new factories. In the towns, the shops were full of cheap, factory-made goods such as kitchenware, clothes, knives and forks, cups and saucers. Although factory work was hard, and often dangerous, most people in Europe and North America believed that they lived in a time of progress.

By the middle of the 19th century, new developments such as railroads, steamships, and gas lighting provided further evidence of progress. Inventions such as the telegraph (1837) and telephone (1876) helped news and information to travel more quickly, and people became increasingly interested in what was happening in other parts of the world. Daily newspapers became big business as they competed to publish the most up-to-date news.

At the time, Britain was the most industrially advanced nation in the world, with the largest overseas empire and the most powerful navy. In 1841, the British were still toasting the health of their young queen, Victoria, who came to the throne in 1837. Victoria reigned for more than 60 years. She was a woman in tune with the spirit of her times, for despite all the talk of progress and advancement, the years around the middle of the 19th century were troubled ones. A series of revolutions and wars, the rapid growth of towns and cities, the sudden appearance of new inventions, a feeling of constant change — all these things made people feel nervous and fearful about the future. To dispel these fears, many people, including Queen Victoria, emphasized the importance of traditional values such as

The opening ceremony for one of the first railroad lines to be built in England, during the 1830s.

Nationalism

Nationalism, a people's belief and pride in themselves as a nation, became an important idea in the 19th century. In South America, nationalism led to several countries breaking away from the Spanish Empire and declaring themselves independent nations. In Europe three new nations, Belgium, Italy, and Germany, came into existence during the 19th century. Traditionally, power in western Europe had been shared among five nations — France, Spain, Portugal, Britain, and the Netherlands. Now there were three more European nations, proud of their nationhood and determined to be treated as equals by the other, older nations.

Simón Bolívar, who spread nationalism through much of South America.

the Christian Church, charity, and family life.

Concentrating on these values helped many people to stop worrying about the future. Some people were inspired to do more. Many organizations were formed with the intention of helping the needy. Some tried to improve conditions at home, and others aimed to help people overseas. Most of the overseas organizations were formed by branches of the Christian Church. Their chief aim was to convert people to Christianity. But some organizations sent doctors and nurses in addition to priests to Africa and other distant lands.

Europeans in Africa

The northern edge of Africa, along the coast of the Mediterranean Sea, has had links with Europe for at least 2,000 years. Inland from this coastal region, the rest of Africa was separated from Europe by the world's largest desert — the Sahara. Until the 15th century, the only contact with Africa south of the Sahara Desert was by camel caravans that trudged slowly across the desert from waterhole to waterhole. The caravans carried cloth, metalwork, and salt southward. In return, they brought back gold and ivory. During the 8th century, this caravan trade came under the control of Islamic Arabs. In the east, the Arabs also ventured southward by sea, establishing fortified trading posts along the coast at ports such as Mombasa and Zanzibar.

The first Europeans to venture south of the Sahara were the Portuguese. Like the Arabs, the Portuguese built fortified trading posts on the African coast. From places such as the fort of São Jorge in Elmina in what is now Ghana, they began to ship black slaves across the Atlantic Ocean to the West Indies and America. Other European nations, such as France, Spain, and Britain, soon

A camel caravan crosses the Sahara Desert.

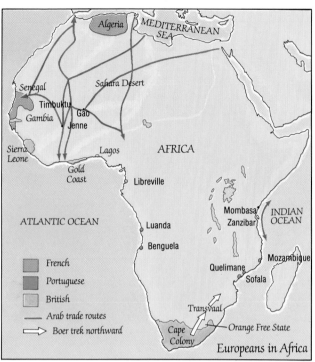

French
Portuguese
British
Arab trade routes
Boer trek northward

Europeans in Africa

joined in this trade, setting up their own bases on the African coast.

Later, some of these bases were enlarged to become colonies. Yet as late as 1870, European possessions in tropical Africa amounted to very little. The Portuguese had long-established bases on the coasts of Angola and Mozambique. The French, too, were well established on the coast of Senegal, and they had an outpost in Gabon. (They also had a major colony, Algeria, in North Africa.) But the British had only a few bases on the West African coast: in Sierra Leone, Gambia, the Gold Coast, and the island of Lagos (in present-day Nigeria).

In 1841, the largest territory in Africa under European control was Cape Colony, situated at the southern tip of the continent. Originally established by Dutch settlers in the 17th century, Cape Colony was taken over by the British at the end of the 18th century. In the 1830s, some descendants of the Dutch settlers, who called themselves Boers, set up what they called the Orange Free State to the north of Cape Colony. During the 1850s the Boers also claimed the region known as the Transvaal.

African exploration

European interest in Africa began to increase in the 18th century, partly as a result of the Industrial Revolution (see page 8). European merchants needed to find new markets to sell the manufactured goods that were made in their factories. They also wanted to find out what raw materials could be obtained in Africa apart from gold and ivory.

In 1788, the Africa Association was founded in London. One of the first aims of the Association was to explore the river systems of Africa, in the hope of finding suitable waterways for transporting goods into and out of the African interior. In 1795, the Association sent the Scottish explorer Mungo Park (1771–1806) to investigate the Niger River in West Africa. Park sailed up the Gambia River and then journeyed overland to reach the Niger. Five years later, Park led a second expedition to the Niger, during which he was killed. In 1827, the French explorer René Caillié (1799–1838) set out across the Sahara Desert in disguise. By pretending to be an Arab, Caillié became the first white person ever to visit the desert town of Timbuktu and return alive. Timbuktu had long been famous in Europe for its great wealth and its isolation. But because it was part of the Islamic world, it had been inaccessible to Europeans.

The Nile River is the only important African river that flows into the Mediterranean Sea, and so it was an obvious target for

The French explorer, René Caillié.

European explorers. As early as 1768 another Scottish explorer, named James Bruce (1730–94), had tried to find the source of the Nile and had reached Khartoum in Sudan. Nearly 100 years later, in 1857, two British men, Richard Burton (1821–90) and John Hanning Speke (1827–64), set out from the East African coast in search of the Nile. Burton was an experienced traveler, and like Caillié, he had spent much time disguised as an Arab. Speke was an ex-army officer. Traveling overland, the two men discovered Lake Tanganyika, which Burton believed to be the source of the Nile. Speke disagreed. A little later, he discovered Lake Victoria while exploring on his own, and he claimed that this was the source of the Nile. Neither explorer would accept the other's theory.

To try to settle the matter, Speke returned to Lake Victoria two years later in 1860. With a companion, James Grant, he searched along the north shores of the lake for a northward-flowing river and eventually found the source of the Nile in July 1862. The Nile River, which at 4,000 miles is the world's longest river, had now been traveled from end to end by white explorers.

The explorer, Richard Burton. He is wearing the oriental robes in which he often disguised himself while traveling.

John Speke pictured by Lake Victoria, which he proved was the source of the Nile River. His gun and surveying instruments are beside him.

Horizons

You could find out about some of the famous people who lived at the same time as Livingstone and Stanley: Charles Dickens (novelist); Giuseppe Garibaldi (Italian nationalist); Florence Nightingale (professional nurse); Thomas Edison (inventor); Karl Marx (political thinker); Abraham Lincoln (American President); Marie Curie (scientist); Isambard Kingdom Brunel (engineer).

Transportation and Equipment

River travel

Africa is a huge continent, stretching almost 5,000 miles south to north, and more than 4,000 miles from east to west at the widest point. Explorers in Africa often traveled across a wide variety of landscapes — lush grassland, sunbaked desert, dense rain forest, and thick swamps infested with millions of biting insects. There were also natural obstacles to overcome — sheer cliffs, steep-sided gorges and canyons, the towering peaks of extinct volcanoes, and many rivers. Some of the rivers were broad, almost a mile across, and slow-moving. Others were narrow, racing torrents that crashed through rapids and plummeted over huge waterfalls.

Rivers were both the key to the exploration of Africa, and the biggest obstacles. From their experiences in North and South America, as well as in Europe itself, Europeans knew that rivers often formed natural highways into the interior of a continent. In Africa, however, the mouths of many rivers were blocked by sandbars or rapids, making it impossible for European ships to sail far upriver.

Many of the African rivers had long been used for transportation by local people in dugout canoes and other simple boats. However, the river journeys made by the local inhabitants were usually over fairly short distances. Both Livingstone and Stanley followed African rivers over hundreds and thousands of miles. By doing so, they were able to trace the geography of the African interior. Whenever

Stanley's collapsible boat, the *Lady Alice*. The *Lady Alice* was originally built in five sections, but they were too large and unwieldy, so Stanley had the boat redivided into eight.

possible, Livingstone and Stanley traveled by boat. They usually bought or hired canoes from the local people, but other types of craft were also used. For his second expedition, Stanley had a special boat that was built in sections. Each section was light enough to be slung between wooden poles and carried by two porters. When fastened together, the eight sections made a boat nearly 40 feet long and over 6 feet across at its widest point. It could carry up to 20 people. Stanley named

Livingstone's first steamboat, the *Ma Robert*.

this boat the *Lady Alice*. The great advantage of this design was that the boat could be carried overland, avoiding the rapids and waterfalls that were a barrier to river craft.

Livingstone used a series of specially built steamboats on his Zambezi expedition. The first steamboat, called the *Ma Robert*, was not powerful enough to move against the current of the river, so he ordered a second, bigger boat. Unfortunately the design was faulty, and a third boat was built. This was named the *Lady Nyasa*. The *Lady Nyasa* was powered by a wood-burning steam engine that was just powerful enough to propel the boat forward at a few miles per hour.

A fisherman paddles his dugout canoe across a lake in Central Africa. Larger canoes can carry 20 or more people.

African craft

Although many of the African peoples had a tradition of skilled wood carving, they built very simple boats. People who lived near water made dugout canoes hollowed from a single tree trunk up to 50 feet long. These dugout canoes were the basic form of river transportation. To make larger craft, rafts were built by lashing logs together. Small, one-person boats were also made from reeds or wooden frames covered with animal skins. The African peoples who lived near the coast used dugout canoes for ocean-fishing, but they did not venture far out to sea. Until European ships arrived in the 15th century, the largest vessels used in Africa were Arab-style dhows that sailed up and down the eastern coast. Many of these dhows were over 80 feet long and could carry large amounts of cargo. Dhows were also sailed up and down some rivers, but they had a much more limited use than canoes. The main reason for this was that dhows were too large to be carried around rapids, waterfalls, and other river obstacles.

On the march

When it was not practical to travel by river, Livingstone and Stanley often rode in oxcarts, or on horseback. However, for much of the time the only way to make progress was by the most reliable means of transportation known to human beings — walking. But

A small dhow sailing down the East African coast.

this did not mean that Livingstone and Stanley walked alone; in fact, they rarely traveled with a party of fewer than 20 people. More often, the exploration party was made up of between 50 and 400 people, nearly all of them local Africans.

Livingstone and Stanley were often the only white people in the exploration party. Some of their African followers were full-time members of the expedition, hired at the start as guards, guides, and interpreters. Others were part-time members who joined an expedition to work as porters for just part of the trip.

An early 20th-century photo of African porters following the white leader of an expedition.

Oxcarts

With careful handling from its African driver, an oxcart could travel over very rough country.

When Livingstone first arrived in Africa, he made several journeys by oxcart. The oxcart is an ancient but reliable means of transportation that is still used in parts of Africa and Asia. The type of cart used by Livingstone was developed by the Dutch Boer settlers. Each cart was pulled by a team of 14 animals, controlled by an African driver who walked alongside cracking a long whip. Carrying up to a ton of goods or supplies, oxcarts made slow but steady progress, averaging about 12 miles per day. In this part of Africa, traveling by oxcart was known as "trekking."

During his early explorations, Livingstone used oxcarts to transport his family around Africa. For weeks at a time, his wife and small children would be packed into carts to trek for hundreds of miles across rolling plains and deserts.

Porters, usually men but sometimes women, were paid little more than their keep to follow the expedition leader. In return they endured hardship and dangers, and carried a load of almost 90 to about 110 pounds, day after day. Without these African guards, interpreters, and porters the white exploration of Africa would not have been possible.

In the 19th century, a well-equipped expedition into Africa required several tons of baggage — supplies, trade goods, clothing, and weapons. Sometimes there were special items such as Stanley's portable boat (see page 12). All of this equipment and baggage had to be divided into bundles of 90 to over 100 pounds and carried by porters.

An explorer's medicine chest, designed by Henry Stanley. Medical supplies were vital to the success of expeditions in Africa.

Supplies — these were usually basic foodstuffs such as bags of rice and dried beans, salt and sugar and, if possible, some tea or coffee. Cooking utensils for the whole expedition also had to be carried. Medical supplies were packed into a heavy medicine chest.

Trade goods — these were essential, because without them no expedition could hope to obtain fresh supplies and the goodwill of the local inhabitants. Few African people used money at this time, so rolls of cotton cloth were traded instead. Porters were often paid with a certain number of yards of cloth per week. An expedition might also exchange rolls of cloth for ivory, or use cloth to buy permission to travel through a particular territory.

Clothing — African people generally wore lightweight clothing, suitable for the hot climate. The white explorers, however, wore almost exactly the same clothes as if they had been in New York or London. As expedition leaders, Livingstone and Stanley were expected to set a particular example. Stanley once lost his

Tropical Hats

Africa was considered to be a particularly dangerous place for exploration. Rugged boots were essential to protect the feet and lower legs against snakes, and to prevent insects from burrowing into the skin. Some form of headgear was also necessary, to protect the explorer's head from the effects of strong, tropical sunlight. Livingstone usually wore a simple peaked cap, while Stanley preferred a specially designed tropical helmet.

The tropical helmet, also called the pith helmet, was developed by the British army in India. The helmet was made of compressed plant fibers (pith), and had a broad sloping brim. For ceremonial use the helmets were colored white, but for everyday use they were covered with pale brown cloth. To improve the cooling effect of the helmet, some manufacturers introduced ventilation tubes that were supposed to let air circulate around the wearer's head under the helmet. Whether this ventilation system worked is doubtful. It did, however, make the helmet even heavier and more cumbersome than it already was.

A much simpler and lighter form of protection was the turban, made from a length of cloth and worn by many people in Sudan and East Africa. But dressing like the African people was an unthinkable idea to most white people at this time.

The tropical helmet worn by Henry Stanley when he "discovered" David Livingstone.

David Livingstone's favorite blue cap, which he wore during most of his time in Africa.

temper with one of his white companions, who went barefoot in front of the African porters.

Weapons — Africa was not a safe place for a small party of travelers. There were dangerous wild animals, and many of the inhabitants distrusted the European explorers, whom they regarded as hostile intruders. Even a missionary such as Livingstone considered a gun to be an essential piece of equipment. Guns were also used to shoot animals for food. However, in Africa, as on other continents, shooting wild animals soon became a sport for rich white people. During his explorations, Stanley carried an elephant gun. This was an extremely powerful hunting rifle that could fire explosive bullets.

Mosquito menace

Rivers may have been the key to the exploration of Africa, but white explorers would not have survived as they traveled along these rivers without the drug, quinine. Human beings in Africa are likely to suffer from a disease known as malaria. This disease is spread by blood-sucking insects called mosquitoes, that live in damp places such as swamps and rivers. Malaria is caused by a tiny organism that can live in human blood. When mosquitoes bite people who have the disease, they transfer the organism to other people they may bite. Malaria kills some people, and makes others suffer from bouts of fever and pain.

In the 19th century, people had not yet discovered how malaria was spread, or what caused the disease. But they had learned that quinine, which is obtained from the bark of the South American cinchona tree, could protect one against malaria. Taken every day, quinine prevents the organism from living in human blood. Livingstone took doses of quinine made to his own recipe, and he encouraged his companions to do the same. Today, drugs based on quinine are still used as a defense against malaria.

Some African peoples have evolved their own natural defense against malaria. Their blood cells are a slightly different shape, and this prevents the organism from living in their blood. The drawback to this naturally evolved defense is that a small percentage of the population have very differently-shaped blood cells. These cells cause the disease known as sickle-cell anemia. Today, many people of African descent suffer from this inherited disease.

This mosquito has nearly drunk its fill of human blood. By feeding in this way, mosquitoes spread the disease malaria.

The Expeditions of David Livingstone

Early travels

David Livingstone landed in Cape Colony, southern Africa on March 15, 1841. He bought an oxcart and made the 480-mile trek to a small missionary settlement called Kuruman, which was situated beyond the northern border of the colony. Kuruman was run by a missionary named Robert Moffat. While he was at Kuruman, Livingstone roamed the countryside, getting to know

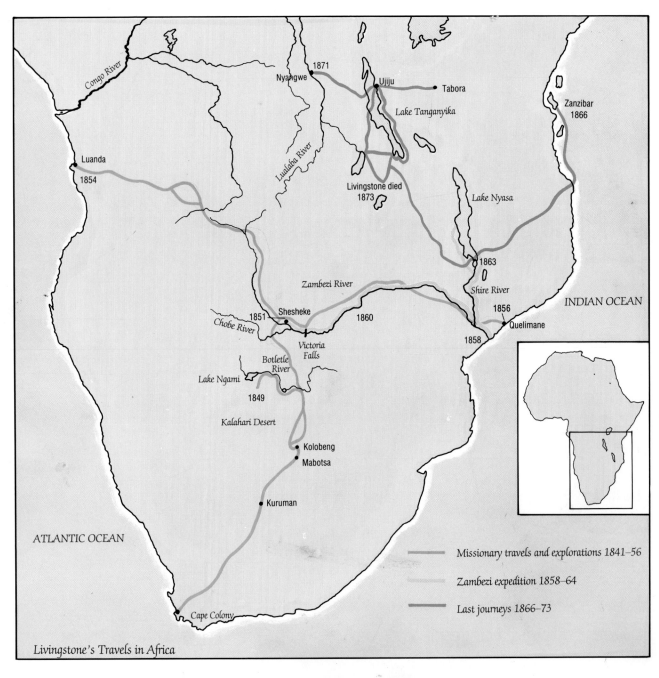

Congo River

1871
Nyangwe
Ujiji
Tabora

Lake Tanganyika

Zanzibar
1866

Luanda
1854

Lualaba River

Livingstone died
1873

Lake Nyasa

Zambezi River

Shire River

1863

INDIAN OCEAN

1851
Shesheke
1860
Chobe River

1856
Quelimane

1858

Victoria
Falls

Botletle
River

Lake Ngami

1849

Kalahari Desert

Kolobeng
Mabotsa

Kuruman

ATLANTIC OCEAN

Missionary travels and explorations 1841–56

Zambezi expedition 1858–64

Last journeys 1866–73

Cape Colony

Livingstone's Travels in Africa

the local Africans and learning their language.

Eventually, Livingstone was given permission to move farther north and start his own mission settlement. He went to a place called Mabotsa where he built a hut for himself and began to get to know the local people. In February 1844, he was attacked by a lion, and his left arm was badly injured. There was no other doctor for hundreds of miles, so Livingstone had to operate on his own arm to make sure that it healed. He endured terrible pain, but he did eventually recover. He then returned to Kuruman where he married Mary Moffat, the daughter of the missionary.

Livingstone was restless. He didn't like working as a doctor, and he wasn't a very good missionary, but he did like traveling. He and his wife moved house twice in the next two years, trekking farther and farther north. The Livingstone family, now including a son and newborn daughter, eventually settled at a village called Kolobeng. Here, they lived in a mud hut until they could build a European-style house.

For a couple of years, the family lived quietly in Kolobeng. By 1848, Livingstone was disillusioned with his missionary work. When the opportunity arose to join an expedition, Livingstone sent his family back to Kuruman. The leaders of the expedition planned to travel across the Kalahari Desert, a region never previously crossed by white people.

The first discoveries

The expedition was financed by two rich white hunters, named William Oswell and Mungo Murray. They were accompanied by Livingstone, five oxcarts, 80 oxen, and 30 Africans from Kolobeng, who wanted to trade ivory obtained from north of the desert. The expedition set out at the beginning of June 1849 and two weeks later was crossing the Kalahari, traveling from waterhole to waterhole and often going thirsty.

On July 4, Livingstone and his companions reached the banks of the Botetle River where the landscape was transformed from bare, dry desert to lush, riverside vegetation. They followed the course of the river, marveling at the variety of birds and animals. Soon the expedition reached Lake Ngami, which was then more than 60 miles long. The size of the lake varies with the amount of rainfall in the highlands of Angola. When visited by another expedition 13 years later, the lake was almost dry.

The Africans living by the lake were friendly, but they would not let the expedition proceed any farther north. So the expedition returned to Kolobeng. Livingstone immediately wrote to London to announce the news of the crossing of the Kalahari and the

In 1849, Livingstone joined an expedition to cross the arid Kalahari Desert.

In 1851, Livingstone took his family with him when he went exploring. Here he is shown walking hand-in-hand with his son, Robert.

discovery of Lake Ngami. Although the hunters financed the expedition, it was Livingstone who got the credit for its success.

In 1851, Livingstone teamed up with Oswell again in order to explore the rivers north of Lake Ngami. This time Livingstone took with him Mary and their three children, despite the fact that his wife was expecting another child. Trekking north by oxcart, Livingstone avoided the Africans near Lake Ngami by taking a different route to reach the Chobe River. Here, Livingstone became friendly with the chief of the Kololo, called Sebituane. Although Livingstone admired Sebituane, he was upset to discover that the African chief sold captured enemies to slave-traders from Angola. This was Livingstone's first real encounter with African slavery.

Sebituane suddenly died of pneumonia, but Livingstone was able to leave his wife and children in Sebituane's village while he and Oswell ventured farther north. On August 4, the two men arrived at the banks of the mighty Zambezi River. The river was nearly a third of a mile wide, and it made a tremendous impression on Livingstone. He wanted to explore it from end to end, but first he had to take care of his family responsibilities. He returned to Sebituane's village, collected his family, and took them back to Kolobeng. In April 1852, Livingstone put his wife and four children on a ship for Britain and waved goodbye.

To the west coast

In June 1852, Livingstone set out on his greatest journey. During the next four years he was to travel more than 5,000 miles, most of it through territory never before seen by a white person. Livingstone now had a new plan for spreading Christianity in Africa. He believed that the African people would only accept

Christianity if the slave trade was replaced by trade in other goods. He therefore wanted to examine the possibilities for establishing trading centers in the heart of Africa, where Europeans would help Africans to grow crops such as cotton for export to Europe.

The first stage of this journey was a northward trek to the town of Sesheke situated near the Zambezi River. Livingstone then planned to follow the Zambezi westward, aiming for the port of Luanda on the Atlantic coast. From Luanda, he would return across Africa and follow the Zambezi downstream to the shores of the Indian Ocean. Livingstone's first destination — the west coast — fitted in well with the ambitions of the Kololo. Sebituane's successor, his son Sekeletu, was eager to trade directly with the slave-dealers on the west coast. So Sekeletu organized a Kololo trading expedition to accompany Livingstone to Luanda.

In November 1853, after some delay, the expedition left Sesheke. While they followed the river, Livingstone and his companions traveled by canoe, paddling hard against the flow of the river. After leaving the river, Livingstone marched overland. He and many of his African companions were ill with fever. The expedition did not have enough food, nor did it have adequate supplies of trade goods to exchange for food from the local people. Finally, in May 1854, an exhausted David Livingstone staggered into Luanda, where he spent several months recovering. In September, he and the Kololo started the return journey and arrived back at Sesheke in September 1855.

Crocodiles and hippos were a constant hazard to river travelers in Africa.

Down the Zambezi

After a few weeks rest, Livingstone continued eastward. On November 16, he became the first white person to see the magnificent waterfall that he named Victoria Falls. At first he considered using the local African name "Mosi-oa-tunya," which means, "smoke that thunders." Only later did he decide to name the waterfall after the British queen.

Continuing along the northern bank of the Zambezi, Livingstone decided to take a shorter route across the healthier uplands rather than to follow the river through mosquito-infested lowlands. While in the uplands, Livingstone made some errors in measuring the height of the land. As a result, he mistakenly came to believe that the lower stretches of the Zambezi could easily be traveled by boat.

The journey was frequently delayed by encounters with the local inhabitants. Many of the Africans were suspicious of the expedition, believing Livingstone and his companions to be slavers. But, with the help of his African companions, Livingstone managed to negotiate a safe passage without violence. On May 25, 1856, after traveling across the African continent, David Livingstone arrived at Quelimane on the eastern coast. Here he rested for two months, then sailed to Britain.

This picture of Victoria Falls shows why the local name for the falls means the "smoke that thunders."

An ill-fated expedition

When Livingstone arrived back in Britain, he found that he had become a national hero. The British people were proud of David Livingstone, the brave missionary explorer. Because of his popularity, Livingstone was befriended by some influential people in the British government. They helped him

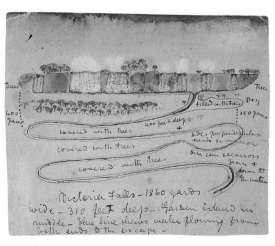

Livingstone's sketch map of Victoria Falls.

to plan his most ambitious expedition so far—to travel by small steamboat up the Zambezi River.

As a result of his mistaken surveying, Livingstone had convinced himself that it would be easy to travel up the Zambezi. At the end of this journey, he intended to set up a trading post in the middle of Africa. Livingstone stayed in Britain for more than a year making preparations for his journey, and writing a book called *Missionary Travels,* which became a best-seller.

In the spring of 1858, Livingstone sailed for Africa in command of a government expedition. He was accompanied by six white assistants, including an engineer to operate the steamboat. From the outset, the expedition was not a success. Although the steamboat (the *Ma Robert*) was able to travel some way up the Zambezi, its path was soon blocked by rapids, which Livingstone had missed on his previous journey through the uplands.

Livingstone decided to explore the Shire River, which flows into the Zambezi. Following this river northward, he came across the lake from which the Shire River flows, Lake Nyasa (now called Lake Malawi). But Livingstone was mainly interested in the highlands around the upper reaches of the Shire River. This was the place, he now thought, to set up a British colony to promote both trade and Christianity. He failed to convince the British government of the need for a colony, but he did persuade a group of missionaries to come from Britain to settle in the Shire highlands. He also ordered a new steamboat.

During 1860, Livingstone traveled overland up and down the Zambezi Valley, revisiting the Kololo kingdom and making many detailed notes about the plant and animal life. Then, early in 1861, a party of missionaries arrived, together with the new steamboat. Unfortunately, the new boat was too big for the shallow parts of

Livingstone's steamboat, the *Ma Robert*, stuck in mud during an unsuccessful attempt to navigate the Zambezi River.

Mary Livingstone with her youngest son, William.

the Shire River, and it could not travel as far as Lake Nyasa, so Livingstone ordered a third, smaller steamboat. He also invited his wife to join him.

While the missionaries established their settlement, Livingstone explored the area around Lake Nyasa. He was upset to find burned villages and other evidence of attacks by slavers. In January 1862, the third steamboat arrived, together with more visitors from Britain, including Mary Livingstone. The expedition was now becoming large and unmanageable, and in addition to constant problems and delays, many of the white people were sick. In April, Mary Livingstone became ill with malaria and despite treatment with quinine, she died.

Although he was greatly saddened by his wife's death, Livingstone tried to carry on with the expedition. The new steamboat was named the *Lady Nyasa* in anticipation of reaching the lake. The many waterfalls and rapids on the Shire River meant that the steamboat would have to be taken to pieces and carried overland for parts of the journey. But although Livingstone made a determined effort to take the steamboat up the river, he was forced to give up. His expedition had dwindled to only a few companions, and the local people, devastated by famine and slaver attacks, were too weak to help. When he did arrive at Lake Nyasa, on foot, Livingstone found that most of the missionaries had died of disease. The whole expedition was a failure. Livingstone sold the *Lady Nyasa* to an Indian merchant, and sailed for Britain. This time there was no hero's welcome.

The last journey

After making arrangements for his children's education, Livingstone returned to Africa for the last time. He was no longer really interested in missionary work. He wanted to check for himself Speke's report of the source of the Nile River, but most of all he wanted to do something about slavery.

In January 1866, Livingstone arrived in Zanzibar, the Arab-ruled island that was a major center of the slave trade. Patrols by British naval ships ensured that fewer slaves than before were exported overseas. But slaves were in demand in Zanzibar itself, so there were still plenty of slavers, armed with guns, raiding the weaker African peoples on the mainland. When they ran into a group of people, the slavers would shoot all the men and capture the women and children. The newly caught slaves were then forced to carry elephant tusks back to Zanzibar. Only about one in five slaves survived the journey. Livingstone formed a curious relationship with the Arab slavers. Although he was strongly opposed to their work, Livingstone became friendly with several Arab traders, and they helped him many times during the following years.

Livingstone sailed from Zanzibar with only a few guards and porters, and after reaching the African mainland, he slowly marched on a roundabout route toward Lake Tanganyika,

David Livingstone with his daughter, Anna Mary, in 1864.

exploring as he went. The expedition pushed westward as far as the Lualaba River, which actually flows into the Congo, although Livingstone believed that it joined the Nile. On July 15, 1871, Livingstone witnessed a violent attack started by some Arab slavers in the town of Nyangwe. Over 400 Africans, mainly women and children, were killed. Livingstone was horrified by this violence, but there was nothing he could do.

Lost and found

Meanwhile, in Britain, Livingstone was largely a forgotten figure. Many people believed that he was dead. The British government was undecided about whether to send a rescue expedition to look for him. But before they could make up their minds, an American newspaper had sent out its own expedition, led by Henry Stanley.

In fact, Livingstone was not lost. He knew exactly where he was, but he was very ill and running short of food and supplies. In one of the most famous meetings in history, Stanley "found" Livingstone at Ujiju, beside Lake Tanganyika, on November 10, 1871. Despite the differences in age and character, the two men liked each other and stayed together for several months. Stanley then returned to Europe to make newspaper history, while Livingstone remained in Africa. Stanley took with him many letters from Livingstone, including one that contained a description of the massacre at Nyangwe. When it was published, this account caused an outcry and helped to focus public attention on the anti-slavery campaign.

In March 1872, Livingstone was once again alone in Ujiju. The supplies that Stanley had brought made Livingstone's life a little easier, but the old explorer was still sick and weak. Nevertheless, he was determined to carry on looking for sources of the Nile. In August, he set out on the march again. Livingstone kept traveling for another eight months, keeping a diary and writing letters, until he died on May 1, 1873, in swamps far to the south of Lake Tanganyika. His African companions carefully preserved his body and carried it more than 1,200 miles to the coast where it was shipped to England. In April 1874, David Livingstone was buried in Westminster Abbey in London. He was mourned by the whole nation as a true British hero.

Susa and Chumah, two African friends who remained with Livingstone until he died and who escorted his body to the coast.

The Expeditions of Henry Stanley

The famous meeting

Henry Stanley's first expedition into Africa was not for exploration — he was a newspaperman on the trail of a story. He set out from Zanzibar with a large party that included two cooks, a Palestinian interpreter, and a group of African soldiers armed with rifles. Led by an African boy carrying the American flag, he took the expedition directly inland, making first for the town of Tabora, and then for Ujiju on the shores of Lake Tanganyika, where Livingstone was believed to be staying. Stanley drove the members of his expedition hard, frequently using a whip to urge them on. When they reached an area of swamp, many of the party became ill with tropical diseases. In less than a month, Stanley himself lost nearly 45 pounds. Nevertheless, he managed to force the exhausted expedition to march the 500 miles to Tabora in just 85 days — 30 days less than expected.

After leaving Tabora, the expedition found its way blocked by a war being fought between Arabs and local Africans. Stanley wanted to force his way through, but after a short battle he was persuaded to make a detour to avoid the fighting. By this time, Livingstone had in fact arrived at Ujiju, where he was recovering from a bout of fever. As Stanley approached Ujiju, the local

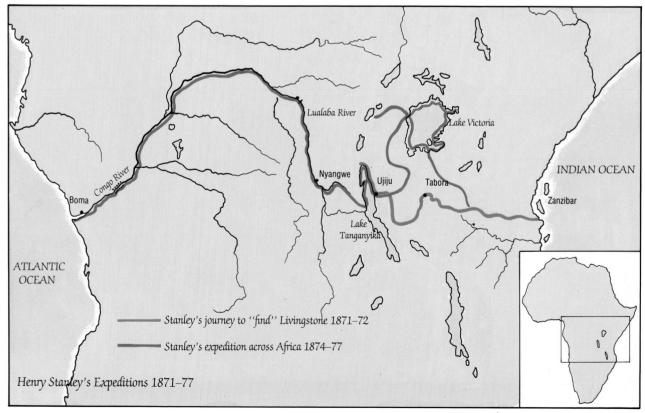

Stanley's journey to "find" Livingstone 1871–72

Stanley's expedition across Africa 1874–77

Henry Stanley's Expeditions 1871–77

people confirmed that a white man was staying there. Stanley knew that he had found Livingstone. Putting on his best clothes and ordering the boy with the flag to the front, Stanley marched noisily into Ujiju to greet Livingstone, who was sitting in a chair outside a hut.

Livingstone stood and nodded at him, and Stanley said the famous words "Doctor Livingstone, I presume?" The two men chatted for a while, but Livingstone was too polite to ask what Stanley was doing in Africa. It was only the following day that Stanley admitted that he had been sent by a newspaper. The elderly explorer was surprised and flattered.

Stanley stayed with Livingstone for five months. The two men traveled slowly around the northern shores of Lake Tanganyika, and Livingstone explained to Stanley how he had almost, but not quite, solved all the puzzles of African geography. When Stanley did return to England, his story, "How I found Livingstone" made him famous. His only problem was what to do next.

"Dr Livingstone, I presume?" The famous meeting at Ujiju.

Across Africa

The answer was provided by two newspapers that wanted to finance an expedition to continue Livingstone's work after his death. Stanley was the obvious choice for leader.

At the time, Stanley's expedition was the biggest exploration project ever organized. Stanley left Zanzibar in November 1874, leading a group of 356 people, including some women and children. He planned to march overland until he found the Lualaba River. Stanley thought that the Lualaba was probably the upper part of the mighty Congo River, although Livingstone had believed that it flowed north into the Nile. To settle the question, Stanley was determined to follow its course downstream to the western coast. Among the numerous items of baggage that he took were the eight pieces that made up the portable boat, the *Lady Alice*.

Once again Stanley drove his expedition hard, even though

Stanley, (center, wearing his tropical hat) surrounded by some of the many Africans who joined his second expedition.

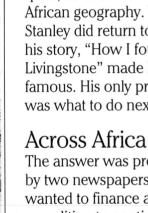

Stanley spent several weeks sailing around Lake Victoria, exploring the shoreline by boat.

African porters hauling canoes up a hillside to avoid a waterfall during Stanley's second expedition.

conditions were harsh. Much of the journey was through hot, dusty plains strewn with thickets of spiky thornbush. The expedition suffered from disease, and was slowed down by opposition from some of the local inhabitants, who did not want to allow such a large and well-armed band of people to roam freely through their lands. By the time Stanley reached Lake Victoria more than three months later, the expedition was reduced to 166 people. About 30 people had died of disease, 24 had been killed in a battle with local Africans, and the rest had deserted, running away at night.

Stanley now ordered the pieces of the *Lady Alice* to be assembled. He sailed around Lake Victoria with a small party, while the rest of the expedition followed along the shore. Near an island at the southern end of the lake, the *Lady Alice* was attacked by some of the local inhabitants. Although none of the expedition was seriously hurt, Stanley still wanted revenge. Some time later he returned to the island in the *Lady Alice*, accompanied by six large canoes. There, he and his men killed 30 of the inhabitants and injured over 100 more.

Leaving Lake Victoria, Stanley led the expedition overland to Ujiju. Another 38 men deserted on the way, and Stanley forced some of the remainder to march in chains like slaves to discourage further desertions. From Ujiju, the expedition sailed around Lake Tanganyika, using the *Lady Alice* and a large, borrowed canoe. At Nyangwe, near the Lualaba River, Stanley reinforced his expedition with 500 porters and armed men hired from local chiefs and Arab slavers.

The expedition continued, following the Lualaba River which, as Stanley had thought, flowed into the Congo. Traveling was extremely difficult, with temperatures as high as 104° Fahrenheit. Most of the journey was through dense, humid, tropical rain forest. Many times the expedition was opposed by the local people. But Stanley did not hesitate to attack anybody who tried to block his progress downstream. He often made use of his elephant gun — one explosive bullet could blow a canoe into fragments. The expedition also had great difficulties with the many rapids and waterfalls that it encountered. Several men were drowned while trying to guide the *Lady*

Alice and the expedition's canoes through these obstacles.

The last part of the journey was a continuous struggle with rapids and waterfalls, and in five months the expedition covered a distance of only 174 miles.

Boots that marched across Africa, belonging to Stanley. Signs of "on-the-march" repairs are clearly visible.

Stanley was finally forced to abandon the *Lady Alice* when he was only 48 miles from the Atlantic coast, and he and his exhausted companions marched the last stage of the journey. The expedition staggered into Boma on August 9, 1877. In his diary, Stanley recorded that the explorers had traveled through 52 waterfalls and rapids, fought 32 battles, and destroyed more than 80 African settlements.

The "smasher of rocks"

Stanley became world-famous for his African adventures, and he was soon hired by Leopold II, king of the Belgians. Leopold saw his chance to establish an overseas empire in the Congo region of Africa, and Stanley was put in charge of this venture. Stanley's main task was to supervise the construction of roads around the rapids on the river. Some distance upstream, where the river was more than 12 miles wide, he was to establish a settlement named Leopoldville (present-day Kinshasa). In addition to the tremendous problems of moving heavy equipment through the rain forest, Stanley had to compete against a French expedition. King Leopold was not the only European ruler who was interested in the Congo.

Stanley drove himself as hard as he drove his men, and completed the task in less than two years. During this time, the African workers gave him the name *Bula Matari* "smasher of rocks," because of the way he dealt with obstacles by using explosives. However, the French had also made good progress. Stanley was forced to settle only on the southern bank of the Congo River, while the French settled on the opposite bank. A few years later, Leopold declared a large region of Central Africa to be the Congo Free State — a misleading name, because it belonged to him personally.

The ambitious Leopold II, king of the Belgians, who wanted to create an empire in Africa.

Rescue mission

A contemporary painting, showing General Gordon about to be killed by followers of the Mahdi.

Stanley made his last expedition to Africa in 1887, when he led a small army to southern Sudan to rescue a local governor. At the time, southern Sudan was supposed to be under Egyptian control. However, there had been a rebellion, headed by an Islamic religious leader known as the Mahdi. In the previous year, the Mahdi's followers had defeated the Egyptians in Sudan and killed their governor, the British general, Charles Gordon, at Khartoum (the capital of Sudan). Now Emin Pasha, the German-born, Egyptian governor of Sudan was reported to be surrounded by Islamic rebels.

Although his final destination was southern Sudan, Stanley planned to travel up the Congo River from the west coast rather than the shorter distance from the east coast. By taking the longer route, Stanley hoped to avoid the Islamic rebels, and to further the territorial claims of King Leopold. In return for assistance from Leopold, Stanley planned to take the expedition through the unexplored rain forest between the Congo River and Lake Albert (now called Lake Mobutu Sese Seko). At Lake Albert he hoped to meet up with Emin Pasha.

Although the expedition was well-armed, with 500 repeating rifles and a machine gun, it was poorly organized. The steamboats that Leopold had provided were now broken down and useless, and the expedition had to march much farther than

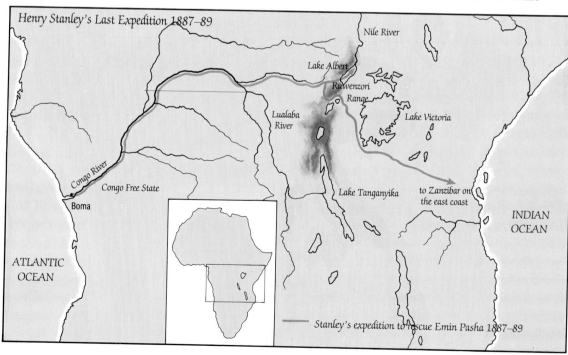

Henry Stanley's Last Expedition 1887–89

Nile River

Lake Albert

Ruwenzori Range

Lualaba River

Lake Victoria

Congo River

Congo Free State

Boma

Lake Tanganyika

to Zanzibar on the east coast

ATLANTIC OCEAN

INDIAN OCEAN

Stanley's expedition to rescue Emin Pasha 1887–89

Mount Speke, one of the snowclad peaks in the "Mountains of the Moon."

Henry Stanley, pictured in the 1890s after he had given up his exploring career.

anticipated. Conditions in the rain forest were extremely difficult, and the party often ran short of supplies. The expedition named one stopping place "Camp Starvation."

As the expedition approached Emin Pasha's headquarters on the shores of Lake Albert, two of Stanley's companions briefly glimpsed a snow-capped peak to the southwest. This was one of the "Mountains of the Moon," now known as the Ruwenzori Range. These were the mountains that the ancient Greeks had heard about 2,500 years ago. The Nile River was said to spring from three lakes that drew their waters from the melted snow off the mountains. Stanley saw the mountains for himself a month later.

By the time the expedition arrived at Lake Albert, after a journey of 13 months, Emin Pasha no longer needed rescuing. Despite his protests, Stanley persuaded him to accompany the expedition to the east coast. Back in Europe, Stanley somehow managed to make the expedition seem a great success, and he became even more famous. He went to live in London and returned to Africa for only one, brief visit. In 1895, he was elected a member of the British Parliament. He died nine years later, on May 10, 1904.

Discoveries and Achievements

An aerial view of the Nile River in southern Sudan.

Africa revealed

As suspected, the rivers of Africa held the key to understanding the geography of the continent. By following rivers, Livingstone and Stanley were able to complete the work of earlier explorers. Away from the coast, the interior of Africa is a massive, sloping plateau. Rain falling onto the plateau drains back to the sea in streams and rivers that lead down to the sea. As a result, the interior of Africa is naturally divided into a number of river basins — areas that are drained by a river system. In eastern Africa, the pattern of drainage is complicated by the presence of several large lakes. As these lakes and rivers were explored, the details of the African interior were gradually marked onto maps.

In one sense, however, Livingstone, Stanley, and many other explorers of Africa walked around with their eyes shut. As white people, both Livingstone and Stanley considered themselves to be superior to the black Africans that they encountered. They expected the African people to be primitive, so that is what they saw. We now know that this attitude is wrong, and that these white explorers failed to appreciate the complexities of African society.

By the 19th century, when Livingstone and Stanley were exploring, much of Europe had experienced the Industrial Revolution (see page 8) and many major advances in science, transportation, and communication. Africa was a land of kingdoms, states, and great trading empires with its own religions, cultures, and systems of government. But Africa had not experienced an Industrial Revolution, and in technological and military terms Western Europe was far more advanced than much of Africa. This helped to give many European explorers their misplaced sense of superiority — and because the people of Africa did not have railroads, or telegraphs, or other such symbols of "civilization," most white explorers dismissed everything about the African people as "primitive" and "uncivilized."

The slave trade

One of Livingstone's reasons for exploring the interior of Africa was to try to set up trade in goods such as cotton to replace the trade in slaves (see page 21). Livingstone was appalled by the sight of slaves being marched by their Arab captors in chains to the slave market at Zanzibar.

These slave chains were brought back to England by Livingstone as proof of the cruelty of the African slave trade.

An African elephant. Slaves were often forced to carry elephant tusks (to be sold for ivory) as they were marched in chains to Zanzibar.

Of course, slavery has been practiced by most peoples at some time during their history. Before the 16th century, most slaves bought and sold in Europe and Africa were used as domestic servants in wealthy households. This changed when the Spanish crossed the Atlantic Ocean and conquered large areas of Central and South America in the 16th century. Other European nations also claimed parts of the Americas and the islands in the Caribbean Sea, which became known as the West Indies. This "New World" was rich in land suitable for agriculture and mineral wealth in the form of precious metals, such as gold and silver. Between the 16th and the 19th centuries, about 20 million Africans were shipped across the Atlantic Ocean to work as slaves on plantations and in mines in the New World. Millions more died in chains during the journey. The effect on the populations of the African west coast was devastating.

The transportation of slaves from the west coast of Africa ended during the 19th century. Slavery was abolished within the British Empire in 1833, and in the United States in 1865. Britain and the United States both established African colonies as homelands for freed slaves. The British colony was called Freetown in Sierra Leone, West Africa; the American colony was neighboring Liberia, which means "free country." However, a flourishing slave trade still operated in East Africa, as Arab traders captured people to be sold at the slave market in Zanzibar.

Livingstone's death reminded people of his lonely struggle against the slave trade in East Africa. The public had been horrified by Livingstone's account of the massacre at Nyangwe (see page 25). Public opinion caused the British government to send a fleet of warships to Zanzibar and, in 1873, under threat of bombardment from these warships, the Arab ruler of Zanzibar abolished slavery within his African territory. Less than a year after Livingstone's death, the great slave market was shut down,

Popular Africa

Livingstone and Stanley both wrote accounts of their experiences in Africa, and many more books were written about them. People enjoyed travelers' tales, and books about African exploration often had the additional excitement of fierce animals and the danger of skirmishes with local Africans.

Professional writers soon began to produce adventure books set in Africa, and these also became popular. The hero of these books was always a white man. Sometimes he was an explorer, and sometimes he was a big-game hunter. As a variation, one writer wrote a book about a white hero who was left in Africa as a baby and was brought up by apes. Created by the writer Edgar Rice Burroughs in 1914, this hero has become one of the most famous fictional characters in the world. There are few people who have not heard of "Tarzan."

The cover of one of the many books written about Livingstone after his death. Note the broken slave chains, signifying Livingstone's contribution to the end of the slave trade.

The writer Joseph Conrad also produced a book set in Africa. Called *Heart of Darkness*, his book is the story of a journey up the Congo River to an isolated trading post. Many people think that Conrad's book, while flawed, gives a more accurate picture of Africa than the Tarzan books, because it reveals the way that Europeans exploited both the country and its people.

never to reopen. The closure of the market did not mean a complete end to slavery in Africa. But once the Zanzibar market was closed, it marked the end of any "official" slave trade.

Empire builders

Stanley was motivated by self-improvement, rather than any desire to change or improve Africa, and he had no special regard for the place or its people. To Stanley, Africa was a place of opportunity — the opportunity to make himself rich, famous, and very influential.

Stanley's greatest achievement was to march into the African rain forest and carve out what was first a colony and later an independent nation. Through the force of his will, and by driving

34

Goods were exported from the Congo in steamboats like this one. This boat has been hauled out of the water for repairs. The crew is posing for the photo.

his workers ruthlessly, Stanley created the Congo for Leopold of Belgium. He was one of many white adventurers who were to shape the national geography of Africa. Although their work is not necessarily approved of today, there is no denying the impact that such men had on African history. Stanley's great rival in the Congo was the French explorer Pierre Brazza (1852–1905). Representing the French government, Brazza set out at almost the same time as Stanley, and with similar intentions. In fact, Brazza beat Stanley to the widest part of the river, and was able to make treaties with the local chiefs before Stanley arrived. As a result, Leopold of Belgium had to be content with territory to the south of the Congo River.

Another empire builder was the British-South African politician Cecil Rhodes (1853–1902), who wanted to spread British influence in Africa. Rhodes made a huge fortune from the diamond mines in South Africa. He had ambitions to extend British rule across Africa from Cairo in the north to Cape Town in the south. This was called the "Cape to Cairo" plan. Rhodes invaded the lands of the Ndebebe and Shona people in southern Africa, and took control of these territories. This new country was named Rhodesia (present-day Zimbabwe). Later, Rhodesia was extended northward to include the territory around Lake Nyasa, known as Nyasaland (present-day Malawi).

Horizons

Exploration was usually done by men, but during the 19th century some women also went exploring in Africa. You could find out about: Mary Kingsley (explored the area around the Niger delta); May Sheldon (nicknamed "Lady Boss" by the Africans, led an expedition to Mount Kilimanjaro); Florence Baker (traveled with her husband across Sudan); Alexine Tinné (explored the Nile south of Khartoum).

The "Cape to Cairo" plan – a cartoon of Cecil Rhodes striding across Africa from Cairo to Cape Town.

The People of Africa

People have lived in Africa since the beginning of human life. The oldest human fossils, bones preserved in rock and soil, have been found in eastern Africa. These human remains date back more than three million years. Scientists believe that human beings evolved in Africa before spreading out to populate the rest of the world, some time during the last million years. The Sahara Desert was formed quite recently, during the last 30,000 years. Since that time, this vast desert has proved to be an effective barrier to the movement of large numbers of people between northern and southern Africa.

The fossil skull of a human ancestor, who lived more than two million years ago. The fossil was found in the Transvaal region of South Africa.

Empires and kingdoms in West Africa

In sub-Saharan Africa, the first Africans to make use of iron were the Nok people. The Nok lived in what is now northern Nigeria, and they had established iron smelting by about 500 B.C. Although a knowledge of iron smelting may have been transported across the desert from the Mediterranean, the Nok people probably developed the technology of working with iron themselves. By the time that Nok society collapsed, in about 400 A.D., iron working had spread to most parts of Africa.

Around 500 A.D., the first towns were built in West Africa. The most important of these were Jenné and Gao, situated inland on the Niger River. Gradually, the number of towns increased. By around 1200, many of these towns had become incorporated into the great empire of Mali, which eventually extended to include the desert trading center of Timbuktu. Farther inland, near Lake Chad, was the smaller empire of Kanem. By the end of the 1400s, both Mali and Kanem had been absorbed into the much larger Songhay Empire that stretched across most of the Sahel region below the desert.

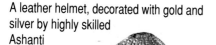

A leather helmet, decorated with gold and silver by highly skilled Ashanti craftsworkers.

Farther south, in the forests of West Africa, separate kingdoms had begun to emerge. In the forest region of Nigeria, the kingdoms of Ife and Benin reached the height of their wealth and power in the 1500s. Artists at the royal courts in these kingdoms produced magnificent bronze statues to adorn the royal palaces. In the 1700s, the power of these kingdoms was eclipsed by the Ashanti state in the forests of nearby Ghana to the west. By this time, however, a new force had arrived on the scene — white traders greedy for the riches of Africa.

Emerging states

By around 1200, metal-working kingdoms had also been established in parts of Central Africa.

The best known of these are Kongo on the Atlantic coast, and Lunda, which was far inland. Around 1600, the Lunda Empire grew in size until it controlled most of the trade in the region.

In eastern Africa, the influence of Islam was very strong, and Islamic Arab traders operated along much of the eastern coast. By about 1000 A.D., several large ports were engaged in trade with India and Arabia. Inland, the construction of Great Zimbabwe commenced around 1200, and it became the capital of a Zimbabwean state. Zimbabwe is the local African word for "stone buildings," and Great Zimbabwe was an impressive series of stone-built enclosures encircling the clay houses of the rulers of the state. To the south, the Sotho kingdoms were established by about 1750. However, these kingdoms were rapidly overshadowed by the rapid expansion of the Zulu state during the 1800s.

There were many other empires, states, and kingdoms in Africa besides the ones described here, although their history is often not well-known. The harsh African climate soon removes most traces of human settlement, and leaves little evidence for later historians. There is much research still to do, and only gradually is the complete history of Africa being revealed.

Farming and herding

Traditionally, most of the African peoples, whether they lived in forest, grassland, or marsh, practiced simple crop farming. African farming was on a small scale, and several different crops were usually grown alongside each other. Traditional African crops such as yams, millet, and groundnuts were widely grown, together with crops such as corn and sweet potatoes, which had

Over much of Africa, farming is traditionally women's work and involves hours of backbreaking labor using hand-held tools.

A Masai man leads his cattle to a waterhole.

A carved wooden mask produced by the Guro people.

been introduced from South America during the 16th century. Much of the farming work was done by women, who also collected wild plants for food and prepared meals.

In parts of eastern and southern Africa, where conditions were suitable, some people lived an existence based on cattle. These peoples, such as the Masai, were wandering cattle-herders. Driving their herds over the plains in search of fresh grassland, the Masai lived on the milk, blood, and meat of their cattle, as well as trading with the local people for other foodstuffs. To the Masai, cattle were the most important form of wealth.

The Tsetse Fly

Large areas of tropical Africa are infested by blood-sucking insects known as tsetse flies. Just as the mosquito transmits malaria, so the tsetse fly transmits a disease called trypanosomiasis. What makes this disease so serious is that it affects both human beings and their domestic animals. In humans, the disease is often known as sleeping sickness, because it makes its victims tired and weak. Horses and mules bitten by tsetse flies die quite quickly, but cattle suffer from a wasting disease known by its African name *nagana*. Affected cattle do not die right away, but slowly lose weight, becoming little more than living skeletons before they eventually die.

Only a few of the upland grassland areas of tropical Africa are free of tsetse flies, and these are the areas occupied by the native cattle-herders. Elsewhere in Central Africa, the tsetse fly makes raising cattle almost impossible.

Natural technology

The first white visitors to Africa noticed the work of the skilled African woodcarvers, who produced ceremonial masks, chairs, and other pieces of furniture. Other craftspeople specialized in making elaborate clothes covered with intricate patterns of beadwork. The woodcarvings and beadwork were thought of as art by these early white visitors. But, at that time, other objects made by the African peoples were dismissed as being "primitive."

Today, people have a much better understanding of African culture, and these "primitive" objects are now widely appreciated. Using natural materials such as grass and reeds, African people created a wide range of nets and traps to catch fish, baskets to carry food and belongings, and mats that could be used as walls, floors, or a roof. Waterproof containers were made from animal skins, hollowed-out dried fruits, and even from ostrich eggs.

Natural materials were also used to make shelters. Traditional African houses are usually built from plant material or clay, or a combination of the two. Timber beams are used to support clay walls, and dried grasses or leaves are used as a roofing material. Many of the houses are circular in shape, with sloping or curved roofs. Each house is surrounded by a small yard area, often containing a separate storage building. From above, many traditional African villages look like clusters of circles, very different from the rectangular patterns of American and European houses and yards.

This grain store in Namibia uses natural materials and the traditional African circular design.

African beliefs

White Christians were not the first missionaries to visit black Africa. Hundreds of years before, Arab merchants traveled across the Sahara Desert and voyaged down the eastern coast, bringing their Islamic religion with them. In parts of East Africa, and in West Africa around the Niger River, the Islamic faith became established among the African peoples. In East Africa, the Islamic influence was reinforced by Arab control of the island of Zanzibar and the nearby mainland.

However, at this time most Africans followed their traditional beliefs. Many African peoples believed that their surrounding environment was alive with spiritual power. Certain plants, both crops and wild species, had special significance and could only be gathered by specific people at particular times. Animals also had great significance in African belief. Wild animals were often considered to be spirit powers, and the cattle-herders believed their animals to be sacred.

In some tribal ceremonies, people danced all day and night until they felt "possessed" by animal spirits.

What Happened Later

Before the interior of Africa was revealed to the rest of the world, European nations were content to have colonies around the coast of Africa. The only major movement inland had been by rival British and Boer settlers in South Africa. But now, in search of new markets and raw materials, other nations began to take an interest in expanding into the interior. Stanley's creation of the Congo Free State for the Belgian king (see page 29) brought the situation of European nations in Africa to a crisis point. Some of the nations that had a tradition of overseas empires, such as Britain and Portugal, objected to Leopold's claims. The French supported Belgium, because they had their own plans for West Africa, and had reached an agreement with Leopold. There were also two newly united European nations — Germany and Italy — that felt entitled to a share of Africa, too.

In 1884, an international conference was held in Berlin, Germany, to settle the problem. The conference decided that Leopold could keep the Congo, and that Africa was to be divided up among the other European nations. This decision began the so-called "Scramble for Africa."

The "Scramble for Africa"
The "Scramble for Africa" lasted only about 20 years. In 1880, less than five percent of Africa was ruled by European nations. By 1900, the whole of Africa had come under European rule with the exception of Ethiopia (then called Abyssinia) and Liberia.

France claimed nearly the whole of western Africa, apart from a few coastal territories, together with the island of Madagascar. French Africa accounted for nearly a third of the continent, from Algeria in the north to Gabon in the south. Britain had the next largest share including Egypt, Sudan, part of Somaliland, Nigeria, Kenya, Uganda, Rhodesia, and most of South Africa. Germany claimed Togo and Cameroon in West Africa, and large territories in southwest Africa (Namibia) and East Africa (Tanzania), while Italy took Libya, Eritrea, and the other part of Somaliland. The Portuguese held on to Angola, Mozambique, and Guinea-Bissau, and the Spanish grabbed the western edge of the Sahara Desert. Right in the center of Africa, now surrounded by other European colonies, was the Belgian Congo.

The nations of Europe drew new borders onto the map of Africa with little regard for the African peoples. Resistance to the Europeans was widespread, but well-equipped armies were sent to fight against the Africans who opposed European rule. Hundreds of thousands of Africans were killed in wars against the Europeans, and millions more suffered hardship, hunger, and disease as a result.

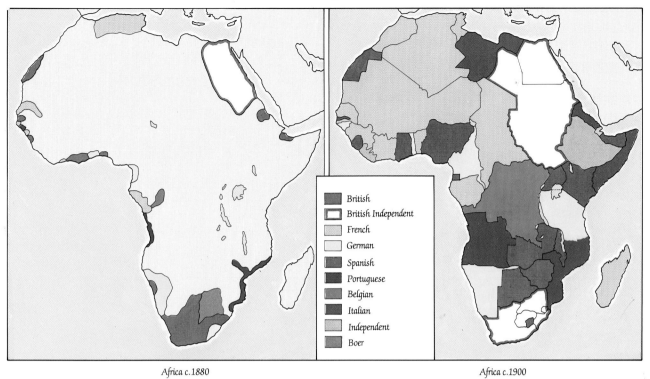

British
British Independent
French
German
Spanish
Portuguese
Belgian
Italian
Independent
Boer

Africa c.1880

Africa c.1900

The "Scramble for Africa"

By the beginning of the 20th century, virtually the whole of Africa was ruled by seven European nations. White settlers did not move to Africa in large numbers, because conditions were too unhealthy and uncomfortable. Typical colonial activities, such as mining and plantation agriculture, relied on cheap African labor. In many of the colonies, farmers were forced by their European rulers to grow crops such as cotton, cocoa, tea, and coffee for export. Raw materials such as cotton were exported cheaply from Africa and manufactured into goods in Europe, some of which were then sold back to Africa for a large profit. For the colonial powers, governing Africa meant producing cheap goods to make a profit, with Africans providing cheap labor. Many Africans were treated little better than slaves.

Big game hunting was a typical white settler's activity during the colonial period in Africa.

20th-century wars

During the 20th century, three wars have influenced the history and political geography of Africa. The South African War (1899–1902) was fought between the British and their rivals, the Boers. After the war, the various territories in southern Africa, both British and Boer, agreed to have a single government. In 1910, the Union of South Africa was formed. In this new nation, only white people were allowed to be part of the government or take part in elections.

The second war started in 1914, when rivalry

among the European nations erupted into open warfare after Germany invaded Belgium and France. This war is called World War I (1914–18), because countries from all over the world became involved. Germany lost the war, and one result was that it also lost all its colonial territories in Africa.

In 1939, Germany invaded Poland, and this was the beginning of World War II (1939–45). At first, fighting was confined to Europe and the Mediterranean, but in 1941 the war spread to all parts of the globe, including Africa. World War II ended when the United States dropped two atomic bombs on the Japanese cities of Hiroshima and Nagasaki. The horrors of this war gave the world a tremendous shock. People began to realize that the world had to change, and the principle that people should have the right to choose their own government began to be widely accepted. In 1945, the United Nations Organization (UN) was formed to promote peace and a decent standard of living for all people.

The idea of nationalism spread, and many people in colonies all over the world began to demand their freedom. Some colonies became independent immediately after the war, but others had to wait for years. In Africa, the process of decolonization was particularly slow. Often, the white inhabitants tried to retain control and resisted attempts to give power to the Africans. In some countries, the African people became impatient with the slow pace of change and began an armed struggle for independence. Over the last 50 years, the nations of Africa have gained their independence and have been admitted to the United Nations. Independence has not always brought peace, however. Several African countries have continued to suffer from internal strife as rival groups have struggled for power.

Jomo Kenyatta being sworn in as president of Kenya, after the country achieved independence from Britain in 1962.

The last outpost

The Union of South Africa became a rich and powerful country in the years leading up to and during World War II. After the war, the white government passed a series of laws that made the black population second-class citizens, with very few rights. In fact, the black people of South Africa had had few rights ever since the birth of the Union in 1910, when the white minority took over most of the land, leaving only a tiny fraction for black South Africans to farm and live on. But these laws "legalized" this unjust system, which was called apartheid.

During the 1980s, protests against white rule in South Africa involved more and more people.

Nelson Mandela at his inauguration on May 10, 1994.

At first, black South Africans protested peacefully against apartheid. But when these peaceful campaigns had no effect, the protests began to become increasingly violent. People everywhere demanded freedom for black South Africans. At the end of the 1980s, the South African government began to release black leaders from jail, and to promise political reform. One of these leaders, Nelson Mandela, had been a political prisoner for 27 years. Finally in 1994, in the only South African election ever open to all races, Nelson Mandela became the first black president of South Africa.

Looking back

David Livingstone and Henry Stanley are sometimes seen as symbols of white involvement in Africa. Livingstone represents the good intentions – the desire to help Africans and to spread Christianity. In contrast, Stanley represents the bad side – greed and a complete lack of respect for Africans and their cultures. But for all their dreams and ambitions, they were just two men doing their jobs, first as missionary and newspaper reporter and later as explorers, enduring hunger, hardship, and disease. As a result of their travels, they opened up Africa to Europe and Europeans.

Horizons

You could find out about the following people and places, which have all played an important role in Africa during the 20th century: Gamal Abdel Nasser (Egyptian president who nationalized the Suez Canal); Soweto (a black township in South Africa); Robert Mugabe (the first president of independent Zimbabwe); Idi Amin (military ruler of Uganda); Haile Selassie (hereditary ruler of Ethiopia); Mau Mau (Kenyan secret society opposed to British rule).

Glossary

Apartheid A system of racist laws used in South Africa until the late 1980s. Under apartheid black people had to live in separate areas and were deprived of most of their human rights.

Boers Descendants of Dutch settlers in South Africa.

colony A territory that is settled and administered by another country.

dhow A traditional Arab boat or ship with a single triangular sail.

Islam The religion based on the teachings of the prophet Mohammed.

ivory The substance that forms the tusks of elephants and some marine mammals.

malaria A human blood disease that is spread by mosquito bites.

massacre The killing of a large number of unarmed people by armed soldiers.

mission A center for religious teaching established overseas in order to spread a particular religion.

mosquito A small, flying insect that feeds by sucking blood from mammals.

nationalism A political idea that emphasises ethnic differences. Nationalism is usually linked to a desire to be free from foreign rule.

quinine A drug obtained from the bark of the cinchona tree which helps prevent malaria.

steamboat A boat powered by a steam engine.

trading post A small settlement established overseas for the purpose of trading with the local population.

trek The Boer word for a long journey by slow-moving oxcart.

workhouse An institution in 18th- and 19th-century Britain where the poor and unemployed could receive shelter and food in return for menial work.

yam The edible root of a tropical plant.

Further Reading

Africa and the Origin of Humans. Raintree Steck-Vaughn, 1988

Arnott, Kathleen. *African Myths and Legends*. Oxford University Press, 1990

Clinton, Susan. *Henry Stanley and David Livingstone: Explorers of Africa*. Children's Press, 1990

Graves, Charles P. *Henry Morton Stanley*. Reprint of 1967 ed. Chelsea House, 1991

Halliburton, Warren J. *Africa's Struggle for Independence*. Macmillan, 1992

Halliburton, Warren J. *African Landscapes*. Macmillan, 1993

Hoobler, Dorothy, and Hoobler, Thomas. *African Portraits,* "Images Across the Ages" series. Raintree Steck-Vaughn, 1993

Humble, Richard. *The Travels of Livingstone.* Watts, 1991

Jones, Constance. *A Short History of Africa, 1500–1900*. Facts on File, 1993

Ofosu-Appiah, L.H. *People in Bondage: African Slavery in the Modern Era*. Lerner, 1993

Packard, Edward. *Africa: Where Do Elephants Live Underground*. McGraw-Hill, 1989

Pogrund, Benjamin. *Nelson Mandela: Strength and Spirit of a Free South Africa*. Gareth Stevens, 1992

Scoones, Simon. *The Sahara and Its People*. Thomas Learning, 1993

Shearman, Deidre. *Queen Victoria*. Chelsea House, 1987

Smith, Chris. *Conflict in Southern Africa*. Macmillan,1993

Index

© Evans Brothers, Limited, 1994